⌒ INTRODU ⌒

Dear Reader

These lines were written to amuse myself, though I trust they amuse you too. I hope they bring back happy memories to older readers, and also, if you aren't that old, that you may be surprised to learn how things were for us in the '20's and '30's.

There have been lots of changes in my lifetime. I recall my family building *"cat's whisker"* wirelesses, and the first time I heard voices coming *"out of the blue"*. My older relatives remember travelling in a horse-drawn coach in Oldham in the early '20's. Such changes as these make me want to write about times past.

I hope this little book brings you pleasure. If it increases your own *"laughter lines"* on a wrinkled face, or even on a younger and smoother one, that will bring joy to me.

Sincerely yours

Contents

Lancashire Laugh Lines

by

Kay Davenport

Cover & illustrations
by
Brian Ormerod

Landy Publishing
1993

Kay has also written and published:-

A Lancashire Hotch Potch	£2.95 plus 30p post
My Preston Yesterdays	£2.00 plus 30p post
Some Oldham Times	£1.75p plus 30p post
Lancashire Hotch Potch: A Second Helping	£3.95p plus 35p post

These are available from the bookshops or from Kay at 1 Canon Flynn Court, Milnrow Road, Rochdale. OL16 5DP.

ISBN: 1 872895 15 8

Published by Landy Publishing
3 Staining Rise
Staining
Blackpool FY3 0BU
Fax/Tel: 0253 886103

Landy Publishing have also published:-

In Lancashire Language: Dialect Poems chosen by Bob Dobson £4 plus 50p post

Valley Verses by Margaret Helliwell. (Dialect Poems and stories) £2.50 plus 30p post

Printed and bound by Galava Printing Company Limited, Nelson, Lancashire

Auntie May's Corsets

Aunt May scorned the nutmeg cure
Swearing that she knew for sure,
That a new potato was the best,
Inside her corset, next to her vest,
She vowed the minerals inside the spud,
Did her rheumatics a power of good.

The potato was removed at night,
Along with clothes and corset tight,
Just before she got into bed,
Giving two lovers the go-ahead
For dalliance in the room below.
The sleepy mother was not to know
The courting couple all aglow
Were listening with ears alert
For the signal they were free to flirt.

My cousin with her sailor friend,
On leave, with little time to spend,
Wished to improve the shining hour,
By smooching with her paramour
Ma had sat with eyelids drooping
Hoping the lad was not for stopping.
Till, with reluctant "*Good Night, God Bless,*"
She retired to bed and to undress.
Pink laced corsets, hard to undo
Modesty vest and bloomers too.

Then the potato hit the lino,
Soon she'd be in bed, and Limbo,
The waiting pair then blessed the spud
Which told them Ma'd retired for good,
In night clothes she'd not descend
To surprise the lass and her Jack Tar friend
The falling potato had indicated
Sport could begin, although belated.

Joy in the parlour, whilst overhead,
Mother asleep in her lonely bed.

Nutmeg In Her Knickers

My friend's Auntie Nora
Kept nutmegs in her drawers
Making dents in her dimpled knees,
When she knelt to scrub the floors.

Modern lassies might well ponder,
Also causing them to wonder,
HOW the nutmegs could remain,
Without them falling out again.
But THEY know only scanty panties,
NOT voluminous ones like Aunties',
At knee and waist elasticated,
Keeping the wearer well protected,
Re-enforced with gusset (double),
Keeping the maidens out of trouble.

Nora, when asked about her bloomers,
Answered, it was fact, not rumours,
That nutmegs were a certain cure,
For rheumatism, t'was for sure,
It was not just an old wives' tale,
A spud, or nutmeg could not fail,
If secreted next the skin
By corset or knickers to keep it in,
Would cure rheumatics or the 'screws',
When confined inside one's trews,
(Wool Combinations would not do,
— Too many slits, so nuts fell through).

Aunt scoffed at girls' bikini briefs,
She swore to her own beliefs
They were too small for the wearers' good,
No room to spare for spice or spud!
(And as for tights and skinny jeans,
— They'd crush the nuts to smithereens!).

She liked her pants with room to spare,
The sort a grandmother should wear,
"Directoire's" the PROPER name
For knee length knickers, all the same
Auntie Nora knew of others,
Known to nineteen-twenties mothers.
(But she would only 'tell the tale'
When fortified with good Brown Ale).

They were 'Passion-dampers' 'Finger-trappers',
Worn by naughty fast-cat flappers.
After a drink, and for good measure,
She told another yarn I treasure,
From old Fred in the USA,
Who wrote to tell how in his day,
Knickers, tight at waist and knee
Enclosing all so cosily ......
Harvest Bloomers they were called
Remembered with joy, now he is old.
Because of the Hymn of Harvest Home
"WHEN ALL IS SAFELY GATHERED IN".

Flaming Nora

"Flaming Nora" - who is she?
On reflection could she be,
The lass in nineteen twenty three,
Burnt to a crisp - (in effigy)
Outside a little Oldham house
For being a lover and not a spouse?
Thus, living well before her time
The punishment had to fit the crime.

So, other women who were jealous,
Making them be over-zealous
Of Nora, who was living tally
Unlike married Jane or Sally
Bored with husbands fat and bald,
Becoming prematurely old,
Unsatisfied in every way
Decided they would have her pay.

They set her effigy alight
Though it wasn't Bonfire night!
They gathered up some ragged clothing,
Venting their envy and their loathing
By making up a guy-like figure
With cackle and with witch-like snigger,
Screaming, *"Nora is a whore"*
Opposite her own front door.

They fanned the flames in cruel fashion,
With hateful and self-righteous passion,
Just because she was unwed
Unpossessed of a marriage bed.

But that was many years ago;
Today, we'd set the skies aglow,
If couples living o'er the brush
Who really see no need to rush
To tie the knot when they can wait
For marriage at a later date.

If likenesses were burnt today,
Of married men who played away,
Our firemen would be occupied
From morning light till eventide!

If girls who take in live-in lovers
To sport and romp beneath the covers,
Were set alight in effigy
How many bonfires would there be?

Fire extinguisher sales would soar,
Smoke alarms too, and what is more
Because of married folk who flirt
FIREMEN WOULD BE ON FULL ALERT!!!

The Golden Age Of Innocence

When innocence was still alive
Way back in nineteen twenty five,
For happy children such as us,
'Neath the elderberry bush,
Or swinging from the apple tree,
Mary, Elspeth, Jess and me,
When all days seemed like summer days
Bright with joy, our Golden Age.

Our minds were then developing,
Questions needed answering,
Auntie had a fine new baby,
Delivered by a stork, or maybe
Brought home in a Gladstone bag,
By the kindly Doctor Spragg.

Sometimes, Cyril joined our gang,
A choirboy, who so sweetly sang,
In St. James's junior choir,
Whose pure young voice soared ever-higher,
Singing of the wings of doves
Or Jesus and eternal love.

Cyril's Grand-dad had a hen-pen
We all played there, now and then.
There was a rooster, and some hens,
Surely Grand-dad could be asked,
How hens laid, and chicks were hatched?
Hens ate broken shells, he swore,
This LEFT us puzzled, as before
He said they then were Mother Hens
The answer really made no sense
For none of us could contemplate
What food expectant mothers ate.

Elspeth questioned cousin Ruth,
Who positively knew the truth,
'A husband gave it to his wife,
It really was the "stuff of life"'.
Their stock was under lock and key,
To keep it safe and warm said she.
'It's white and fluffy well wrapped up,
In bathroom cupboard, two shelves up.'
Each promised to investigate
Their medicine cabinet.

I'd have to stand upon a chair
Just to discover what was there,
Then, reaching in, I found the stuff
And it **was** fluffy, sure enough,
All well wrapped up in paper too,
But paper of a faded blue.

This stuff of life was orange-red,
NOT white as cousin Ruth had said,
The puzzle then had not been solved,
For the moment it was shelved.
Forgotten as we played at 'shop',
Hopscotch, skipping, whip and top.

Soon Winter came, with colds and chills,
Rheumatism, other ills.
Chests were rubbed with smelly goose-grease,
Sometimes bringing much relief.
Steamy footbaths hued like custard,
By a tin of Colman's mustard,
On the rag-rug by the fire side
Gave relief to feet so tired.

One night Dad stripped to his vest
Rubbed Wintergreen upon his chest,
Mother went upstairs to get
The orange stuff from the cabinet,
She plastered it upon Dad's side
I stared and wondered goggle-eyed
At this homely fire-side scene
As I sipped by Ovaltine.

I struggled through my catechism,
Dad groaned with his rheumatism,
Could this be *"The stuff of Life?"*
The secret gift twixt man and wife
Then I learned the proper name
Of this balm the shade of flame.

My Dad stretched and sighed and said
"Come on Mother, time for bed."
He seemed cured now, all serene
AND HE PRAISED THE NAME OF THERMOGENE.

The Nun's Tale

Sister Anne, in contemplation
Praying for the World's salvation
In the chapel of the convent
At eventide when all was silent
Graceful candles all alight
Silver sconced so pure and white
The altar light glows rosily
Symbolic of eternity

Sister Anne feels old and weary
Yet, sees in mental eye so clearly
Though mind meanders back and forth
Through the years twixt age and youth
A little light of long ago
Orange-yellow, burning low
From humble, stubby tallow candle
In a jam jar with string handle
Double-looped for carrying
For use when she went scurrying
As a little child of four
From the open kitchen door
To the privy in flagged back yard
Trying really very hard
To hide her childish night-time fear
Of bogey-men who might lurk near

Father had made the tiny lantern
For comfort when she felt uncertain
He waited by the kitchen door
So she would really feel secure
Holding there another light
To guide her safely in the night
Into her warm and cosy home
Where she would seldom be alone

The outside closet, like a cell
So small with damp and whitewash smell
A gap below the bolted door
(Her feet had scarcely touched the floor)
(Perched in solit'ry confinement)
No toilet roll—no such refinement
But squares cut from the Daily Mail
Hanging with string from rusty nail
The flick'ring candle in the jar
Shining like a little star
Had given comfort, calmed her soul
As she watched the white brick wall
Wary of spiders on the crawl

Sister Anne ... Now eighty three
Wonders just why it should be
That her mind drifts easily
Back to life of other days
Remembering that candle's rays
And parents who were good and kind
Now so much upon her mind
Back and forth her fancies wander
From convent's hush to home back yonder

Her mind, now lucid sees the flame
Constant, shining in HIS name
'Neath the cross, beside the altar
Which, like her faith, will never falter,
She does not know the call has come
For entry to her final home
Her heavenly father close awaits
To bear her safely through the gates

Gentle nuns, with quiet pace
Find her in their holy place
A smile of peace is on her face
As if she has a wondrous dream
The waxen candles softly gleam
But the altar light is extra bright
Banishing shadows of the night.

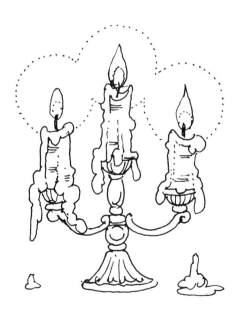

13

Hot Seat

Uncle Teddy, rough and ready
The landlord of an Oldham pub,
Lamed from the *'War to end all war'*
Was serving soldiers in forty-four
With pints of Oldham Brewery beer
Amber coloured, strong and clear,
Thought it not so much as comical
Rather that it was ironical
That maybe he had fought in vain
As Britain was at war again.

Laughter was a rare commodity
Even tales of an outside lavat'ry,
Lads on leave, and everyone
Liked to have a bit of fun,
Though Uncle Teddy was the victim
(Auntie told me this verbatim).

On blackout night with sirens wailing,
The only guide an iron railing
To lead to the tiny outside loo
Where a man must do what a man must do,
Sometimes sitting, often standing
In the closet on an outside landing.

Toilet rolls were not provided,
Newspapers were so divided
In little squares tied to a hook,
Sometimes torn from a comic book
Perhaps from a *'Peg's Paper'* Mag,
Or a Lancashire local rag.

In the darkness, sight unseen
No telling where the squares had been,
Teddy, ready for departing
Found his rear-end badly smarting,
Felt that he was all aflame
Yelled out loudly to his shame
'I'm all afire, I'm all red hot'
As down the passage-way he shot,
Over gas-mask, spittoon, kit-bag
Little bow-legs all a zig-zag.

As he thundered up the stairs
Auntie guessed the fault was hers,
For she had filled the pepper pot
With Co-op pepper strong and hot,
Using a rolled-up paper cone
(The paper square was not alone)
But one of many in a stack
For privy usage - out the back.

The culprit knew it made good sense
To protest her innocence,
But later chortled - *'Well, I guess*
He got the news hot off the Press'.

The Co-op ... The Front Shop

The Rochdale Pioneers of old,
Could really never have foretold,
There'd be Islamic lessons read
Where once we purchased daily bread;
Where Mazawattee tea was bought
Truths from the Koran are taught.

As first the Co-op shops were small,
Then they got bigger, one and all,
Till shopping habits felt the change
To supermarkets bright and strange.
Redundant shops became deserted
Some of them became converted
To temples and religious places,
For immigrants of other races.

Shopkeepers from Middle East
Showed us East and West could meet,
They sold Chapattis, Chillies, Humus
To us indiginous consumers,
Who thought the foreign food exotic
(Some even found it quite erotic!)

A few shops were preserved, to show,
What they were like so long ago.
Tourists, from China and Japan
Call to see where it all began.
The little shop in old Toad Lane
Where good men served for little gain,
Combining, for the common good
Thus keeping down the price of food.

The Jubilee year is almost here,
Co-ops hundred and fiftieth year,
Those of us who reminisce
Recall our local stores like this ....

The Co-op windows were all a-clutter,
With blocks of lard, and tubs of butter,
Tea in packets, salt blocks too,
"Force" wheat flakes, then fairly new,
Whose advertising campaign feature
Was Sunny Jim a funny creature
In coat of red and waistcoat yellow,
Jumping high o'er fence to show
How "Force" gave him a heathy glow.

It raised him up so very high,
That he could almost touch the sky,
Dolls could be obtained like him
Pigtailed, monocled like Jim
(Still available today
Two tokens and two pounds to pay).*

Shoppers came to buy or chat.
Mums, at home had time for that;
Though others worked hard in the mills
To earn the cash to pay the bills
The "Store" sold all but the kitchen sink,
Every kind of food and drink.

To help the shoppers, and boost the trade,
Every effort to please was made
So, horsedrawn carts would make a stop
To pick up parcels from the shop,
Clogs for irons, boots for mending
Customer-service was never-ending;
There was laundry for the well-to-do,
Funeral wreaths could be ordered too,
By mourners or neighbours who collected
Coppers for the flowers selected,
Then they all went on display
In the Co-op shop till the funeral day.

Coal was ordered by the sack,
Trencherbone, ovoids, nutty slack.
Poor coal seemed to burn like slate,
It was two and eight a hundredweight.
'Best' produced blue spurts of gas
Poor stuff yielded piles of ash.

The more a shareholder would spend
Thus increased their dividend.
Each one had a Co-op number,
A different number to remember.
They were never-to-be forgotten
Like army numbers from days of yore.
Brain imprinted for evermore.

Co-op yellow checks were proffered
In exchange for money offered
For every large or small account,
All noted down - the right amount
With pencil of indelible blue,
And carbon paper to keep all true.

A top check, a narrow yellow slip,
Was placed, with moistened finger tip
On gummed sheet so that it would stay
Safe and sound till Quarter Day.

Two bob in the pound, the dividend,
Giving extra cash to spend
On necessary alarm clock
Or p'raps a pretty Whit-walk frock.
The Co-op was a way of life
For shoppers, be it man or wife.
Then, customers were always right,
Assistants tried with all their might,
With friendly smile, or simple joke,
With gossip and suburban talk,
To run a cheap and happy store
So customers would come for more.

Shops, instead of a till for money,
Had cash dispensers worked by pulley,
Coins were placed in small brass cup
The counter hand then winched it up
Pulling a lavat'ry-chain-like handle,
The cup went swaying all a-dangle,
Travelling by overhead wire
Speedily to the lady cashier.

One of many stories told,
Which happened in the days of old,
Concerns a lad who sent a token,
Telling of his love unspoken,
By placing in the cup of brass
Chocolate drops for his pretty lass,
To wing along the tautened wire
Safely to his heart's desire.

But other lads just for a lark
Played a trick on the counter clerk,
Wrapped a cow's eye in silver paper
Thinking it a proper caper;
The girl unwrapped the bogus sweet,
Thinking it a lunch-time treat,
Saw the brown eye all a-glare
(Lucky it was not a pair!)
The lurking fellows - being horrid,
Yelled - *"Here's looking at you kid!"*
Just as Humphrey Bogart did.
In "Casablanca" to sweet Ingrid.

Another story (often told)
Of a woman buying a toilet roll
For visitors had come to call,
Was told the price had been increased,
Up from fourpence to sixpence each,
"I've only fivepence here" she said ....
"Give us two panshiners then instead!"

The Rochdale men were not to know
A hundrèd and fifty year ago,
From the Toad Lane shop's inauguration,
That there would spread to every nation
International co-operation
Deserving of our jubilation.

* Some Sainsbury's obtain them - there's one in Denton.

WHEAT FLAKES

MADE FROM WHEAT, FLAVOURED WITH SUGAR, SALT AND MALT

The Co-op - The "Back Shop"

When Gracie Fields was *"Nobbut a lass"*
And Grandad a little sprog,
Times were hard in Lancashire
In the county of the clog
There was no *"Coronation Street"*
Or even television,
No Co-op Shopping Giant then
But little *"Stores"* for thrifty men,
Pioneered in Gracie's town
By Rochdale's men of vision.

When unemployment stalked the land
And times were really bad,
Those safe in work were envied,
So a lucky *"Flour lad"*
If fired with ambition
Might better his position,
Rise to *"Counter assistant"*
And if he were persistent,
His wage would rise from one pound then,
To manager's wage of four pounds ten!

The Co-op shops between the wars
Had tiled or sawdust covered floors;
There was a *"front shop"* and a *"back"*
With sugar measured from a sack;
The backshop was the lad's domain
Weighing flour self-raising and plain.

He bagged-up both sugar and spice,
Peas, lentils, pearl barley and rice;
There were firewood bundles, oily and dusty,
Tied round with twists of wire so rusty;
Paraffin drums were there as well,
Vinegar barrels with pungent smell.
Housewives came with jugs and with cans,
Lads had often to wash their hands,
For they had to handle cleaner goods
As well as pounds of dirty spuds.
The spuds were weighed in a metal scoop,
When they came hurtling down the chute;
Small babes, as I've oft' heard tell,
Were weighed in the iron scoop as well,
Proud Mammas of babies new
Looked on fondly - and others too;
Some with envy - but others not
For they'd enough with those they'd got.

Pond'ring as the weights were jiggled
"Thank God it isn't mine," they giggled!
But Mum was glad that her baby bunting,
Was weighed in the scale and not found wanting!

Once a flour lad all of fourteen
Bright and cheerful and very keen,
Left in charge temporarily
Had to go out to the W.C.;
He returned, dismayed to see
A customer waiting impatiently.
She questioned just where he had been
And asked him if his hands were clean
"Boy" she asked *"'as thi 'ands bin weshed?"*
"No" said young Kelly, all abashed,
"Then wesh 'em, and look sharp" she said,
He scrubbed his hands till they were red;
He made sure his nails were clean
Up to her standard of hygiene.
He showed his hands for her to see;
Would she want butter, lard, or tea?
He hoped she would not ask for cheese,
So hard to weigh it just to please.
"Reet" she said, *"Now tha can serve me,*
Ah'm allus feart o' germs yo' see.
They're everywhere, the little blighters,
Give us a bundle o' wood ... and two firelighters!!"

The Brownies' Revenge

In Proud Preston Town, of Guild renown
As a child of eight
I learned to hate and **retaliate.**
A **good** girl at school,
I obeyed every rule,
A God-fearing child, gentle and mild,
Each Monday night,
Faces shiny and bright,
Our well-behaved gang,
Frolicked and sang,
Encircling the room,
Round a giant mushroom,
And perching upon it, round eyed, with a scowl
A stuffed tawny owl.
A silent bird who ... n'er said *"Twit to Woo"*,
Centre of attention, oh did I mention?
We were the Brownie Pack, of St. James's Preston.
These are the words ... always the same
"We're the Brownies, Here's our aim,
Lend a hand and PLAY THE GAME!"
OR ....
"We're the fairies, bright and gay,
Helping others on their way".
In separate patrols, (they were called sixes)
Of Gnomes and Elves, Fairies and Pixies,
We learned to tie knots, all stringy and tight,
Pulling together with all our might,
Sheep shanks, clove hitches, all secure,
Should come in handy ... that's for sure.

In half built homes on half-finished streets,
Wishing no harm to man or beast,
We held little picnics, many a feast.
With pebbles and marbles we played at *"shop"*
Innocent, happy ... but brought to a stop,
By a beast in a bowler and his mangy dog,
Watchman, unofficial, with shouts and brass whistle,
Bearing down on us, waving his stick,
Dog barking and leaping, vicious and quick.
Screaming we ran Meg, Jess, Elspeth and me,
O'er half-built walls were forced to flee.

Skirting the lime pit, Elspeth went flying,
Jess scraped her legs, All of us crying,
It's all true ... not rumours,
One wet her bloomers!

So our games ended, afraid, undefended,
The gang held a Pow Wow, all wondering **how**.
How to pay back for the vicious attack,
Should we be meek, and turn the cheek?
No, Pow Wow decreed, **avenge** the foul deed.

So, we collected what we required,
A box from Dad's boots newly acquired,
Bought from the shop, the one with the sign -
"Jackson's hats and boots are **fine**
Ten and six and three and nine."

Then cord from an orange box, hairy and thick,
For good Brownie knots, should do the trick.
Brown paper was easy, always to hand,
But the final ingredient had to be planned.
Armed with Blackpool buckets and spades
We all lay await in the park's leafy glades,
Waiting for Dolly the milkman's horse,
For what she'd drop, as a matter of course.

We waited for her and her steaming load,
Like brown whole-wheat buns dropped in the road
Manure for the roses of Mr. Slade,
Ever-ready with garden spade,
But we spritely Brownies pushed him away,
We thought that our need was greater that day.
We outsmarted the man, collected our booty,
Cried with glee as Doll did her duty.

Dad's boot box was filled, we all were thrilled,
As we packed in the stuff, quite warm, just enough,
The box lid came next, then the brown paper,
We crowed with delight ... oh what a caper,
Now for the string, all hairy and strong,
Soon he'd arrive, he shouldn't be long.
Quick, the knots, we couldn't go wrong!

We were **experts**, at reefs, and clove hitches,
We finished the parcel, (Jess was in stitches).
We posted a look-out, just after five,
Knowing that soon the foe would arrive.
Umbrella swinging, bowler on head,
Fat Mr Browning, a man to dread.
Boots slapping down like ready money,
Strutting along (we thought him so funny).

We'd put the *'present'* right in his path
Hid by a gate, and tried not to laugh.
Not long to wait, would he take our bait?
He gave it a poke with black umbrella,
Then scooped it up smartly, a curious fellow
For ever after .... just for a joke,
We gave him a nickname - *'Mr POKE-POKE'*.

Our gift he bore off under his arm
Off to his bungalow, cosy and warm
We knew he'd struggle, hoped he'd be able
To untie the knots at his tea table.
We pictured his face as he saw what he'd got
Were we repentant? .... not a jot
Satisfied .... We didn't feel bad.
We'd pencilled a message *"Ever been had?"*

We skipped and we sang the next Monday night
A rapturous band of Brownies so bright.
Singing so blithely with all our might
—*"We're the Brownies here's our aim ...*
LEND A HAND AND PLAY THE GAME."

This Is Not A Dress Rehearsal

"He's got to go afore I do
Ahv got some proper living t'do;
Ah wanna live to please missen
Go to Bingo nah an then,
Go on a bus ride when Ah like,
Ride pillion on me gran'son's bike;
Ah want sum money o' mi own
Not doled out meanly wi a frown;
Mi life's been 'ectic - never dull,
Wi a husband like a ragin' bull.
Ah said this years ago and meant it
"It's MY turn now and Heaven sent it".
Yes, it really is my turn
Ah don't think Ah'm too old to learn
Ah want a life wi' peace an quiet
Mi married life 'as been a riot;
Ah want no feet beneath mi table,
Ah'll live by missen whilst Ah'm able,
Ah'm tired o' scraping, scrimping, fratchin,
An' a jealous 'usband allus watchin;
He didna want me out o' seet
Ah tended to 'im day and neet;
It were bring me this an' fetch me that
He hadn'a good word fer t'dog or t'cat
'E thowt good manners didna matter
'E were a pain all wind an watter.
Trousis wi' arse end a-flappin
All that *could* drop were a-droppin'
A reet cantankerous owd sod
But Ah'm as fit as a butcher's dog;
An Ah'm ready to fling me clog
O'er *"Pots an' Pans"** an' Blackpool Tower.
It's goin' to be MY happy hour
Now me fam'ly's gone Ah'm feart o' nowt,
Ah'm free, an' owing no-one owt.
Ah'll be there on all the 'trips'
Wi other widows, on planes and ships
I'll spend his insurance money,
Ah'm off to weer the skies are sunny.
Ah've gorra lot o' living t' do
God gi' me strength
Now Ah'm EIGHTY-TWO."

*"Pots an' Pans" is a hill on the Saddleworth side of Oldham.

Eeni-Meeni-Myni Mo

Eeni Meeni Myni Mo,
If you had chilblains on your toe,
The cure was in the enamel po
— Not filled too high or filled too low.

Feet were dipped into the urine,
For twenty minutes soaked therein.
Then the chilblains lost there shine
Eeni meeni, your feet felt fine!

Eeni meeni myni mo,
Posh folk, with chilblains red and hot
Used a **china** chamber pot
With roses painted on its bottom,
Eeni meeni — some with a lot on.

Each pot was handled, for easy carrying
Necessary for careful emptying
When the article was full,
Eeni meeni, — simply frightful!

The 'pot' was used to save chaps scurrying
And women too, embarrassed, hurrying,
Down to the outside W.C.
What a bother that could be
Eeni meeni, for the sake of a wee.

Eeni meeni myni mo, the hoi-poloi who used a po,
Kept it hidden beneath the bed
Sometimes, a man with a careless tread
Would strike the thing with a heavy bang
Eeni meeni — what a clang!

Eeni meeni each "*guzzunder*"
Had to be pushed so it went under,
Not too far, and not too near,
If too near, why then, I fear
A hanging bedspread got a soaking.
Mothers felt it so provoking
Not a cause for jest or joking
Eeni meeni — yet MORE washing!

Eeni meeni, if out of reach
A worried child would crawl beneath
In haste, might overturn the pot
It was for certain that he got
A hiding as fluid soaked the lino
Eeni meeni, what a crime-o!

Eeni meeni, careful housewives
Trying to live healthy lives,
Used Jeyes Fluid to disinfect,
Or sure as fate she could expect
That a pot whose bottom once had gleamed
Would show wear and tear if left uncleaned
The enamel would go rough and briny
Where once it had been white and shiny
Eeni meeni — scaled and limey.

Eeni meeni, wives in suburbs
Hid *"guzzunders"* in bedside cupboards.
Poorly-paid housemaids did their duty:
The article was a thing of beauty.
They washed and perfumed the painted pot
Making certain there was not
Anything to cause objection.
Eeni meeni — such perfection!

Eeni meeni myni mo, thinking back so long ago
When chamber pots, or poes, were used
In bedrooms, with no privacy
Had folk no sensitivity?
Did honeymooning folk divide?
One in the room, and one outside
Were couples uninhibited
Not bothered when exhibited
Doing what really must be done
— And to hell with love and fun?
Eeni meeni myni did it prevent performance?
Eeni meeni myni did it put a stop to romance?
Eeni Meeni Myni ..... NO!

Manure-Cure

Old Bet from Bardsley had an uncle,
And when he had a ripe carbuncle,
Down to the farmer's field he'd go
And visit Buttercup or Flo.

Patiently he'd stand and wait,
Leaning on a five-barred gate,
Recalling being young and fit,
A miner, then, in Bardsley pit,
Not in need of a bovine cure
Flo, or Buttercup's manure.

Sometimes, Joe remembered childhood,
Home-cures, Ma swore did them good,
She said old remedies were best.
Like camphor, rubbed upon the chest.
Heat-reducing Febrifuge;
Parrish's Food, the shade of rouge.

Nip-bone, made from Cumphrey leaves;
Brimstone and treacle; Yarrow teas;
Syrup of Figs for constipation,
Friars' Balsam for expurgation;
Or Carters' Little Liver Pills;
Beechams' Powders to cure all ills.

When Joe was a baby, for vaccination,
Lymph of Calf for immunisation.
Strange to think, that even now
He hoped for a cure from the end of a cow!

So, for the boil upon his neck,
He knew for certain, and by heck
That Buttercup or Flo's cow-pat
Freshly dropped, like a flat brown hat
Made into a little poultice
So rank, his pals would often notice
That Joe was not the sweetest chap
When plastered well from Flo's cow-pat.

Joe liked his compress warm and fresh,
Wrapped in rag upon his flesh.
To hide the smell he wore a muffler
(Like Job he was a patient suff'rer.)

But Joe, one day when in his field,
Waiting for Flo the cow to yield
Her beneficient remedy,
Quickly collected for his tea
A crop of 'mushrooms' growing free.

So ends the tale of Bet's old uncle,
Although cured of his carbuncle,
Very sadly to relate,
Botulism sealed his fate;
He died from toadstools that he ate.

Bet thinks, upon looking back,
Joe should have visited the Quack
Who would have given him the pills
For any geriatric ills
And, like Flo's off'ring would be free
For a man of eighty-three.
Then, perhaps, he'd be alive,
Going on for eighty-five.

29

Five Inches Of Bath-water

George the Sixth, in wartime decreed
That when we bathed, there was no need
To fill the bath up to the brim,
A gallon or two was enough for him;
He said that for the kingly scrub
A line be drawn on the royal tub;
Five inches high, no more nor less
And for the Queen, and each princess.

Commoners too, must play their part,
And take economy to heart
When filling bath, of tin or zinc,
The hoi poloi must stop and think
Of soldiers, or sailors away at sea
And must conserve all energy.
So all should draw a watermark
Be he aristocracy or clerk.

A man who had a skinny rump
Fared better than one who was plump;
Water rose higher on his torso,
Essentials were covered - only more so!

When I was a girl, just out of school,
Father insisted we keep the rule;
Friday night was the bathtime treat,
But we were allowed to wash our feet
In a bowl, beside the fire,
We bathed our knees, and even higher.

In nineteen forty, a winter's night,
Black-out blind was drawn down tight,
Listening to ITMA, cosy and snug,
Tin bowl filled up, on our rug;
My sister Elsie, home from work,
Was standing on one leg, like a stork,
Soaping her foot, in the brimming water,
When Dad came in and upset his daughter;
She overbalanced, hit the sideboard
Then mother (who was also floored).

The dog was drenched, the peg-rug too,
Dad's legs got washed in the hullabaloo,
Soapy water soaked Elsie's dress
I pondered as I cleared the mess,
How we had saved on heat and water
Royalty could not do better.

We'd washed the dog, the lino too,
Clothes, feet, legs (and mother too)
For doing as King George decreed.
Conserving, for our country's need.

I wondered if he, or 'Lillibet',
And Margaret, or Queen Elizabeth,
Washed their feet by a sulky fire,
Soaping their legs (or even higher)
Got knocked for six, by a tipsy sire?

Dad had to account for our to-do,
When he returned, tin hat askew;
Coming home from his spell of duty,
Doing his bit for King and Country.

His A.R.P. Post had a quiet night,
And he was every-so-slightly tight,
There'd been no sirens, no bombs to fear
The pub nearby had got some beer.

So a warden or two had 'chanced their arm',
Thinking that they could do no harm,
For often, pubs were closed up tight,
A sign on the door *'No Beer Tonight'.*

So Dad was forgiven, we all felt good,
And clean, and careful, as we should,
For each and all had played their part
And taken King George's words to heart,
And though the scene had been chaotic
At least we all felt PATRIOTIC.

31

Make Do And Mend

The Queen was in the sewing-room
Dainty feet a-treadle,
Piecing royal bed-sheets
Neatly, sides to middle.

This was a thrifty custom
For needy busy wives,
But scarcely to be credited
In wealthy royal lives.

War, the greatest leveller
Made all of us the same,
Kings and Queens and commoners
Were players in the game.

When Edward chose to abdicate
For love's young dream, however late,
When Mrs Simpson called the tune,
George was forced to take the throne.

The propaganda war machine
Showed pictures of his lovely queen,
Sitting, like Goldilocks serene,
As she sewed a fine long seam.

In different ways we all contrived
To work and fight to stay alive;
The slogan was 'MAKE DO AND MEND'
For there was little cash to spend.

Coupons were in short supply,
So Royalty and we must try,
Daily to economise,
On shoes and clothes of every size.

A pair of flannel pants of Dad's
Would make two pairs for little lads;
And Mother's bloomers cut in two
Made knickers for Joanne and Sue.

A long coat, fur-trimmed of Mum's
Made coats for sister and two chums,
Re-cycling now is nothing new,
We grandmas know a thing or two.

Sleeve tops from a woolly sweater,
Made bob-caps, and even better

The lower ends made woolly mitts
Sewn to make them perfect fits.

Silk knickers made from a parachute,
Were hard to sew and cold to boot,
Trimmed with lace they could be glam'rous
Delighting soldiers who felt am'rous!

Instead of stockings, sun-tan lotion
Was slapped on legs to give the notion
That a girl's legs were silken-clad
To turn the head of any lad.

An eye-brow pencil came in handy,
To draw a seam all fine and dandy;
The trouble was, if it should rain,
Legs needed painting once again!

There was little make-up then to buy,
Powder and scent in short supply,
Ends saved from rare lipsticks
(A new one made from five or six)
Melted down o'er a low gas-jet
Then poured in a case where it could set.

Lard was used for a softer skin,
Cakes baked with liquid paraffin;
We ate whale-meat oily and tough,
Strange fish tried, like Russion "snoek",
Horse meat eaten by the unwary,
(Dad marvelled at the tasty gravy!)

A propaganda poster read,
'BE LIKE DAD, KEEP MUM' it said;
Feminists were horrified,
"No-one keeps US!" they crossly cried;
"To say Dad does so's hardly sporting,
When war time girls are self-supporting."

"We do our bit for King and Country
And try so hard to keep our beauty,"
They almost were incensed to riot,
The slogan just meant "Please keep quiet."
In case a spy was lurking near,
And secret plans might overhear!

There were dreadful times, and happy too.
We all recall what we went through,
There was all to win and all to do
When we were young in 'Forty-Two'.

Sunday Best

When we all dressed in *"Sunday Best"*
The Sabbath was a day of rest;
The clothing that we wore on weekdays
Was changed for special dress on Sundays,
Boots, or heavy clogs exchanged
For smarter footwear, light and strange;
It was as if we walked on air
Shedding off our workday care.

Fathers wore their pin-striped suits
Collars, ties, and lace-up boots,
Waistcoats, watch-chains, bowler hats,
Gloves and grey, pearl-buttoned spats;
Mothers' coats were trimmed with fur
Or edged with braid for Sunday wear;
Children all felt spruce and clean,
Somehow better, all serene,
Did different dressing make us so?
When we were young, so long ago?

If we should sing a song on Sunday,
Mother said *"This isn't Monday,*
On weekdays sing of Love in Bloom
The Sabbath needs a different tune,
Sing 'Jesus bids us shine
With a pure clear light
Like a little candle
Burning in the night.'
A Temperance ditty's quite alright
Perhaps ... 'My drink is water bright'".

My brother liked to take a chance,
Leading Mother quite a dance;
Oft' on weekdays he would sing
Of Henry Eighth, the cruel king,
Gross, much-married, void of charm,
And Anne, with head beneath her arm,
Who nightly 'Walked the Bloody Tower'.
"It's not a swear-word", Sidney said,
"Queen Anne truly lost her head.
She really walked the Bloody Tower."

Outsmarted, furious, Dad would glower;
Sid got away with it on weekdays
But should he try it out on Sundays
Punishment was swift, I fear,
Sidney got a good thick ear!

For in our homes in byegone days
Children had to watch their ways;
Parents orders were the law
When we were little, long ago.
For swearing, be it son or daughter
Got a mouth wash ... soap and water.

When my pal Frederick was nine
And Sunday shopping deemed a crime
Back in nineteen twenty-three,
His Uncle came for Sunday tea;
Gave the lad a shilling bright,
Such a present, such delight.
To a lad whose joys were few
He planned with care just what to do;
He'd buy four lots of sweets, and so
Treat all the family at a go.

Four little bags, four little treats,
Jelly babies, mint ball sweets
Sugar Almonds, Yorkshire mixtures.
He'd forgotten Father's strictures
That Sunday shopping was a sin.
He waited till his Pa came in,
(Father was a Local Preacher
Not, I fear, a **gentle** teacher).

The gifts were handed out with joy
By the thoughtful little boy,
Father, furious, made a fuss
'Sunday shopping's not for us'
Threw the toffees on the fire
Scowling, watched the flames leap higher,
Frederick was very sad
Feeling guilty, feeling bad.

The tears he's still remembering
Now he is "Decembering".

An Old Rochdale Masher

Long ago he smelled of Brylcreem,
Now his scent is Wintergreen;
Once his teeth were strong and bright,
Now he takes them out at night;
Just to clean, I must explain,
He always pops them in again;
He'd not be seen without his nashers,
Whose youth-day club was 'Rochdale Mashers'.
His Northern pride sustains him still,
Though often he feels tired and ill.
He's still smart and neatly dressed,
Collar clean and trousers pressed;
Dignity must be maintained,
And good grooming still retained;
For now he is *"Decembering"*
.... Remembering.

On steep Drake Street and other places,
Blitheley going through their paces,
Handsome lads and lasses fair,
On Sunday nights with time to spare,
Paraded each town's *"Monkey Run"*,
All hoping for a bit of fun;
Immaculate in Sunday best,
On their only day of rest;
Dull Monday coming all too soon,
Followed by Life's afternoon.
Gathered rosebuds do not last,
Youth and beauty fade so fast,
Now it's all *"Decembering"*,
.... Remembering.

But memory's eye is bright, not sad,
Recalling he was *"quite a lad"*,
That girls gave him the old Glad Eye,
On Falinge Road when he passed by,
In 50 Shilling Burton's suit,
With waistcoat and watch-chain to boot;
Hair so black, like patent leather,
Now it's white, and all a-feather;
Eyes not bright, but still alert,
Knowing he's too old to flirt
With nubile lasses jigging by,
He's much too sensible to try.

There are lady OAP's for sure,
But they have not the same allure,
Tho' bravely some are *"Golden Girls"*,
With fancy frocks and blue-rinsed curls;
In their hearts too they're young and bold,
Like him, refusing to feel old;
He's full of wistfulness, not lust,
It's really that he's just ...... *"Decembering"* ...... Remembering.

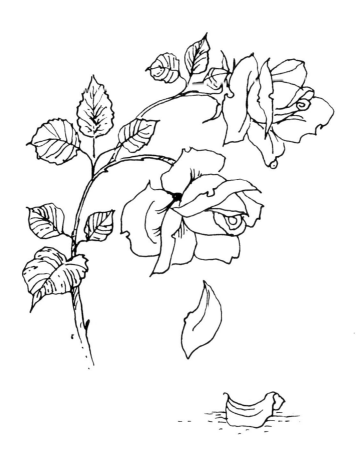

The Old Girls' Dinner
(at the 1992 Preston Guild)

At The Park School Old Girls' Dinner,
A lot of us were fatter,
Just a few were thinner,
Than in the Fifties and it's sure,
Some knew the twenties, and before.

About three hundred Park School Girls,
Now in fancy frocks and pearls,
Many proud of being *"Winckles"*,*
Now grey-haired, and slightly wrinkled;
Powdered, perfumed, rememb'ring too
When schoolgirl make-up was taboo.

Some Old Girls now recollected
How hands and faces were inspected,
By a mistress at cloakroom door,
For a powdered nose, and what is more,
A prefect (some of whom we loved)
Made certain that our hands were gloved,
That panamas were eyebrow straight,
Stocking seams aligned, not bent,
Before we left the upper school
Order mark ... if you broke the rule,
To collect three and you would be
Before the Head or her Deputy.

The Committee who arranged the do,
Had collected photo's, a blazer too,
An old straw hat, a hockey stick,
Boots, pads, knickers and gymslip,
So we could see just as we were,
When we were young, and all to dare,
When navy bloomers were *"de rigueur"*
Gym-slips, pleated to hide the figure.
There also had to be no space,
It was considered a disgrace,
If fleshy strip became exposed
'Neath knicker-leg and woollen hose.

Miss Booth would issue a detention,
Also a lecture, and would mention
That such a gap was called *"a smile"*
Right for Can-Can, but not OUR style.
It surely did not make her grin,
Or schoolgirls who were then kept in.

38

The dinner was good, the speeches fine,
Fortified with food and wine
The noise at times was quite stupendous,
Three hundred voices, quite horrendous,
Recalling this, remembering that.
More schoolgirl talk than 'Granny' chat,
Not feeling middle-aged, or old,
Just being young, and brash, and bold.

Alas, t'was many moons ago,
When we were surely not to know,
Just what the future held for us,
Of sadness and of happiness,
For some are now *"Septembering"*
And quite a few *"Decembering"*.

* "Winckles" was the affectionate nickname given to pupils of
Park School in Preston's Winckley Square.

An Oldham Girl

Once her hair was blonde and crinkly,
Now she's grey, her skin is wrinkly;
Still she's smart, and always dapper,
For she was an Oldham flapper,
When the Charleston was the rage,
And she was twenty years of age;
Linking arms with other lasses,
Trusting lads to make their passes,
"Clicking", *"Trapping-off"* was fun,
When adult life had just begun;
Parading Oldham's Union Stret,
It was the Sunday evenings' treat;
After chapel, dressed to kill,
Forgetting workdays at the mill,
For now she is *"Decembering"*
...... Remembering.

Recalling being young and spry,
The thrill of watching lads go by,
All attired in Sunday best,
Out for romance like the rest.

But that was many years ago,
When she paraded to and fro
With other lassies of the town,
Stepping lightly up and down;
Clogs discarded, for the day,
On the only day of play;
Forbidden make-up on her face
(Ma thought lipstick a disgrace,
"It's sure to lead to hanky-panky"
Must be removed with spit on hanky).
Could it have been so long ago?
When hearts were young and all aglow?
And now she is *"Decembering"*,
...... Remembering.

It lifts her heart today to see,
Lovers pass, so bright so free,
Strolling slowly, hand in hand,
She's not envious, you understand;
For she is *"Decembering"*
...... Remembering.